Daily

Gratitude

Journal

Leia Luana
Copyright © 2021
All rights reserved

This Book Belongs To -

Today I Am Grateful For

Date

Today I Am Grateful For

Date

What gets you excited about life?

Today I Am Grateful For

Date

Today I Am Grateful For

Date

"Be thankful for what you are now, and keep fighting for what you want to be tomorrow."

Today I Am Grateful For

Date

- ♥ _____
- ♥ _____
- ♥ _____
- ♥ _____

What is your favourite emotion to feel?

_____

Today I Am Grateful For

Date

- ♥ _____
- ♥ _____
- ♥ _____
- ♥ _____

- ♥ _____
- ♥ _____
- ♥ _____
- ♥ _____

Today I Am Grateful For

Date

What do you love most about the current season?

_____

Positive Affirmations

- ♥ _____ ♥
- ♥ _____ ♥
- ♥ _____ ♥
- ♥ _____ ♥

Today I Am Grateful For

Date

Today I Am Grateful For

Date

Write down one good thing that happened to you today.

Today I Am Grateful For

Date

Today I Am Grateful For

Date

"No matter how hard life can get,
go to bed grateful for all you have."

Today I Am Grateful For

_____
Date

- ♥ _____
- ♥ _____
- ♥ _____
- ♥ _____

What is the one thing that made me smile today?

_____

Today I Am Grateful For

_____
Date

- ♥ _____
- ♥ _____
- ♥ _____
- ♥ _____

- ♥ _____
- ♥ _____
- ♥ _____
- ♥ _____

Today I Am Grateful For

_____
Date

What do you really appreciate about your life?

_____

Positive Affirmations

♥♥

- ♥ _____ ♥
- ♥ _____ ♥
- ♥ _____ ♥
- ♥ _____ ♥

Today I Am
Grateful For

Date

Today I Am
Grateful For

Date

What about nature are you grateful for?

Today I Am
Grateful For

Date

Today I Am
Grateful For

Date

"I am thankful for nights that turned into mornings, friends that turned into family, and dreams that turned into reality."

Today I Am Grateful For

Date

- ♥ ....
- ♥ ....
- ♥ ....
- ♥ ....

How am I better today than I was yesterday?

....

Today I Am Grateful For

Date

- ♥ ....
- ♥ ....
- ♥ ....
- ♥ ....

- ♥ ....
- ♥ ....
- ♥ ....
- ♥ ....

Today I Am Grateful For

Date

What did I read or listen to today that added value to my life?

....

Positive Affirmations

- ♥ ....
- ♥ ....
- ♥ ....
- ♥ ....

Today I Am Grateful For

Date

- _____
- _____
- _____
- _____

- _____
- _____
- _____
- _____

Today I Am Grateful For

Date

What activity did I most enjoy today?

_____

Today I Am Grateful For

Date

- _____
- _____
- _____
- _____

- _____
- _____
- _____
- _____

Today I Am Grateful For

Date

"One of the greatest gifts you can give someone is thanking them for being part of your life."

Today I Am Grateful For

Date

- _____
- _____
- _____
- _____

What was the most delicious thing I ate today?

_____

Today I Am Grateful For

Date

- _____
- _____
- _____
- _____

- _____
- _____
- _____
- _____

Today I Am Grateful For

Date

What beauty did I see today?

_____

Positive Affirmations

- _____
- _____
- _____
- _____

Today I Am Grateful For

Date

- ....
- ....
- ....
- ....

- ....
- ....
- ....
- ....

Today I Am Grateful For

Date

What was one small victory I had today?

....

Today I Am Grateful For

Date

- ....
- ....
- ....
- ....

- ....
- ....
- ....
- ....

Today I Am Grateful For

Date

"Happiness comes when we stop complaining about the troubles we have and offer thanks for the troubles we don't have."

Today I Am Grateful For

Date

- ♥
- ♥
- ♥
- ♥

What positive emotions did I experience today?

Today I Am Grateful For

Date

- ♥
- ♥
- ♥
- ♥

- ♥
- ♥
- ♥
- ♥

Today I Am Grateful For

Date

What is one positive thing I can say about today's weather?

Positive Affirmations

- ♥
- ♥
- ♥
- ♥

Today I Am Grateful For

Date

Today I Am Grateful For

Date

What made me feel energized today?

Today I Am Grateful For

Date

Today I Am Grateful For

Date

"The best way to be happy is to turn the negatives into positives. Don't let anyone steal your joy and be thankful for what you have."

Today I Am Grateful For

_____

Date

- _____
- _____
- _____
- _____

What is one of your favorite songs from your childhood?

_____

Today I Am Grateful For

_____

Date

- _____
- _____
- _____
- _____

- _____
- _____
- _____
- _____

Today I Am Grateful For

_____

Date

Describe a family tradition that you are most grateful for.

_____

Positive Affirmations

- _____
- _____
- _____
- _____

Today I Am Grateful For

Date

Today I Am Grateful For

Date

What is the one thing that made me smile today?

_____

Today I Am Grateful For

Date

Today I Am Grateful For

Date

"When some things go wrong, take a moment to be thankful for the many things that are going right."

Today I Am Grateful For

Date

_____

What is the one thing that made me smile today?

Today I Am Grateful For

Date

Today I Am Grateful For

Date

What is the one thing that made me smile today?

Positive Affirmations

Today I Am Grateful For

Date

Today I Am Grateful For

Date

What is a recent purchase that has added value to your life?

Today I Am Grateful For

Date

Today I Am Grateful For

Date

"If the only prayer you ever say in your entire life is thank you, it will be enough." — Meister Eckhart

Today I Am Grateful For

Date

What is the biggest lesson you learned in childhood?

Today I Am Grateful For

Date

Today I Am Grateful For

Date

How is your life more positive today than it was a year ago?

Positive Affirmations

Today I Am Grateful For

Date

Today I Am Grateful For

Date

What is your favorite part of your daily routine?

Today I Am Grateful For

Date

Today I Am Grateful For

Date

"Gratitude makes sense of our past, brings peace for today, and creates a vision for tomorrow"
— *Melody Beattie*

Today I Am Grateful For

- ♥ _____
- ♥ _____
- ♥ _____
- ♥ _____

Date

What is your favorite food you love to indulge in?

_____

Today I Am Grateful For

- ♥ _____
- ♥ _____
- ♥ _____
- ♥ _____

Date

- ♥ _____
- ♥ _____
- ♥ _____
- ♥ _____

Today I Am Grateful For

Date

What is one positive thing you can say about today's weather?

_____

Positive Affirmations

- ♥ _____
- ♥ _____
- ♥ _____
- ♥ _____

Today I Am Grateful For

Date

- ....
- ....
- ....
- ....

- ....
- ....
- ....
- ....

Today I Am Grateful For

Date

What is one aspect of your health that you're more grateful for?

_____

Today I Am Grateful For

Date

- ....
- ....
- ....
- ....

- ....
- ....
- ....
- ....

Today I Am Grateful For

Date

"I have a lot to be thankful for. I am healthy, happy and I am loved." – Reba McEntire

Today I Am Grateful For

* _____
* _____
* _____
* _____

Date

Who can you count on whenever you need someone to talk to?

_____

Today I Am Grateful For

* _____
* _____
* _____
* _____

Date

---

* _____
* _____
* _____
* _____

Today I Am Grateful For

Date

What is your favorite habit and why it is an important?

_____

Positive Affirmations

* _____
* _____
* _____
* _____

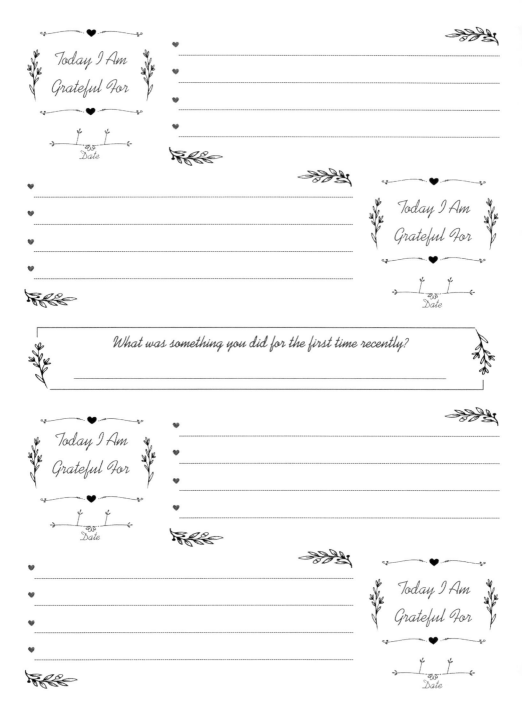

Today I Am Grateful For

Date

Today I Am Grateful For

Date

What was something you did for the first time recently?

Today I Am Grateful For

Date

Today I Am Grateful For

Date

"When you practice gratefulness, there is a sense of respect toward others." – Dalai Lama

Today I Am Grateful For

Date

- ....
- ....
- ....
- ....

What recent memory makes you smile the most?

_____

Today I Am Grateful For

Date

- ....
- ....
- ....
- ....

- ....
- ....
- ....

Today I Am Grateful For

Date

What was the last thing that made you laugh out loud?

_____

Positive Affirmations

- ....
- ....
- ....
- ....

Today I Am Grateful For

Date

Today I Am Grateful For

Date

What is a great recipe you've prepared that others rave about?

Today I Am Grateful For

Date

Today I Am Grateful For

Date

"Thank you for life, and all the little ups and downs that make it worth living." – Travis Barker

Today I Am Grateful For

- ....
- ....
- ....
- ....

Date

Describe a recent time when you truly felt at peace.

_____

Today I Am Grateful For

- ....
- ....
- ....
- ....

Date

- ....
- ....
- ....
- ....

Today I Am Grateful For

Date

What do you love to practice?

_____

Positive Affirmations

- ....
- ....
- ....
- ....

Today I Am Grateful For

- ....
- ....
- ....
- ....

Date

- ....
- ....
- ....
- ....

Today I Am Grateful For

Date

What is a small win that you accomplished in the past 24 hrs?

_____

Today I Am Grateful For

- ....
- ....
- ....
- ....

Date

- ....
- ....
- ....
- ....

Today I Am Grateful For

Date

"Gratitude is not only the greatest of virtues, but the parent of all the others." — Marcus Tullius Cicero

Today I Am Grateful For

Date

- _____
- _____
- _____
- _____

What is your favorite season and what do you like about it?

_____

Today I Am Grateful For

Date

- _____
- _____
- _____
- _____

- _____
- _____
- _____
- _____

Today I Am Grateful For

Date

What makes you beautiful?

_____

Positive Affirmations

- _____
- _____
- _____
- _____

Today I Am Grateful For

Date

_____
_____
_____
_____

_____
_____
_____
_____

Today I Am Grateful For

Date

What are you most looking forward to this week?

_____

Today I Am Grateful For

Date

_____
_____
_____
_____

_____
_____
_____
_____

Today I Am Grateful For

Date

"When I started counting my blessings, my whole life turned around." – Willie Nelson

Today I Am Grateful For

Date

- ♥ _____
- ♥ _____
- ♥ _____
- ♥ _____

What is your favorite time of the year?

_____

Today I Am Grateful For

Date

- ♥ _____
- ♥ _____
- ♥ _____
- ♥ _____

- ♥ _____
- ♥ _____
- ♥ _____
- ♥ _____

Today I Am Grateful For

Date

What activity do you enjoy most when alone?

_____

Positive Affirmations

- ♥ _____
- ♥ _____
- ♥ _____
- ♥ _____

Today I Am Grateful For

Date

Today I Am Grateful For

Date

What activity do you enjoy when with others?

Today I Am Grateful For

Date

Today I Am Grateful For

Date

"The thankful receiver bears a plentiful harvest." – William Blake

Today I Am Grateful For

Date

_____
_____
_____
_____

How have you recently cared for your physical wellbeing?

_____

Today I Am Grateful For

Date

_____
_____
_____
_____

_____
_____
_____
_____

Today I Am Grateful For

Date

How have you recently cared for your mental wellbeing?

_____

Positive Affirmations

_____
_____
_____
_____

Today I Am Grateful For

Date

Today I Am Grateful For

Date

What's something you wish you had done earlier in life?

Today I Am Grateful For

Date

Today I Am Grateful For

Date

"Appreciation is the highest form of prayer, for it acknowledges the presence of good wherever you shine the light of your thankful thoughts." – Alan Cohen

Today I Am Grateful For

- _____
- _____
- _____
- _____

Date

What book are you most grateful for having read?

_____

Today I Am Grateful For

- _____
- _____
- _____
- _____

Date

- _____
- _____
- _____
- _____

Today I Am Grateful For

Date

What hobbies would you miss if you could no longer do them?

_____

Positive Affirmations

- _____
- _____
- _____
- _____

Today I Am Grateful For

- _____
- _____
- _____
- _____

Date

- _____
- _____
- _____
- _____

Today I Am Grateful For

Date

Where was your last vacation? Describe what you did there.

_____

Today I Am Grateful For

- _____
- _____
- _____
- _____

Date

- _____
- _____
- _____
- _____

Today I Am Grateful For

Date

"Let us be grateful to the mirror for revealing to us our appearance only." – Samuel Butler

Today I Am Grateful For

Date

- _____
- _____
- _____
- _____

What is missing in your life?

_____

Today I Am Grateful For

Date

- _____
- _____
- _____
- _____

- _____
- _____
- _____
- _____

Today I Am Grateful For

Date

What is something that you've recently fixed?

_____

Positive Affirmations

- _____
- _____
- _____
- _____

Today I Am
Grateful For

Date

_____
_____
_____
_____

_____
_____
_____
_____

Today I Am
Grateful For

Date

How can you continue being more thankful?

_____

Today I Am
Grateful For

Date

_____
_____
_____
_____

_____
_____
_____
_____

Today I Am
Grateful For

Date

"Gratitude changes the pangs of memory into a tranquil joy." –
Dietrich Bonhoeffer

Today I Am Grateful For

Date

....
....
....
....

What makes you happy when you're feeling down.

....

Today I Am Grateful For

Date

....
....
....
....

....
....
....
....

Today I Am Grateful For

Date

What gift did you enjoy receiving in the past year?

....

Positive Affirmations

....
....
....
....

Today I Am Grateful For

Date

- ....
- ....
- ....
- ....

- ....
- ....
- ....
- ....

Today I Am Grateful For

Date

What freedoms are you most grateful for?

_____

Today I Am Grateful For

Date

- ....
- ....
- ....
- ....

- ....
- ....
- ....
- ....

Today I Am Grateful For

Date

"Gratitude is the most exquisite form of courtesy." – Jacques Maritain

Today I Am Grateful For

Date

♥ ....
♥ ....
♥ ....
♥ ....

Look around the room & list the items that you're grateful for.

....

Today I Am Grateful For

Date

♥ ....
♥ ....
♥ ....

♥ ....
♥ ....
♥ ....
♥ ....

Today I Am Grateful For

Date

What is your top goal?   Why is this goal important to you?

....

Positive Affirmations

♥ ....
♥ ....
♥ ....
♥ ....

Today I Am Grateful For

Date

Today I Am Grateful For

Date

Who do you sometimes compare yourself to?

_____

Today I Am Grateful For

Date

Today I Am Grateful For

Date

"There's no happier person than a truly thankful, content person." – Joyce Meyer

Today I Am Grateful For

- ....
- ....
- ....
- ....

Date

What's the most sensible thing you've ever heard someone say?

_____

Today I Am Grateful For

- ....
- ....
- ....
- ....

Date

- ....
- ....
- ....
- ....

Today I Am Grateful For

Date

What life lesson did you learn the hard way?

_____

Positive Affirmations

- ....
- ....
- ....
- ....

Today I Am Grateful For

- _____
- _____
- _____
- _____

Date

- _____
- _____
- _____
- _____

Today I Am Grateful For

Date

What do you wish you spent more time doing five years ago?

_____

Today I Am Grateful For

- _____
- _____
- _____
- _____

Date

- _____
- _____
- _____
- _____

Today I Am Grateful For

Date

"No duty is more urgent than that of returning thanks." – James Allen

Today I Am Grateful For

Date

- ....
- ....
- ....
- ....

What meals do you most enjoy making or eating?

....

Today I Am Grateful For

Date

- ....
- ....
- ....
- ....

- ....
- ....
- ....
- ....

Today I Am Grateful For

Date

Who do you love and what are you doing about it?

....

Positive Affirmations

- ....
- ....
- ....
- ....

Today I Am Grateful For

Date

Today I Am Grateful For

Date

What things do you own that make life easier?

Today I Am Grateful For

Date

Today I Am Grateful For

Date

"Strive to find things to be thankful for, and just look for the good in who you are." — Bethany Hamilton

Today I Am Grateful For

Date

_____
_____
_____
_____

Do you celebrate the things you do have?

_____

Today I Am Grateful For

Date

_____
_____
_____

_____
_____
_____
_____

Today I Am Grateful For

Date

Have you done anything lately worth remembering?

_____

Positive Affirmations

_____
_____
_____
_____

Today I Am Grateful For

Date

- ....
- ....
- ....
- ....

- ....
- ....
- ....
- ....

Today I Am Grateful For

Date

Which activities make you lose track of time?

_____

Today I Am Grateful For

Date

- ....
- ....
- ....
- ....

- ....
- ....
- ....
- ....

Today I Am Grateful For

Date

"The trick is to be grateful when your mood is high and graceful when it is low." – Richard Carlson

Today I Am Grateful For

Date

_____
_____
_____
_____

If you had to teach something, what would you teach?

_____

Today I Am Grateful For

Date

_____
_____
_____
_____

Today I Am Grateful For

Date

What would you regret not fully doing or having in your life?

_____

Positive Affirmations

_____
_____
_____
_____

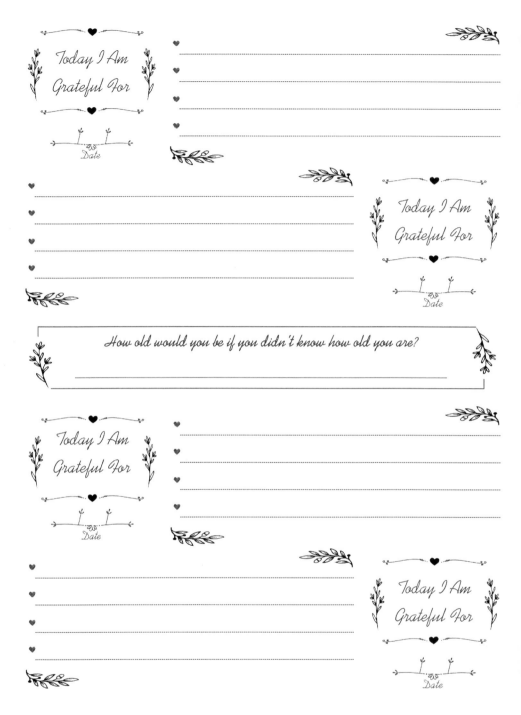

Today I Am Grateful For

Date

Today I Am Grateful For

Date

How old would you be if you didn't know how old you are?

Today I Am Grateful For

Date

Today I Am Grateful For

Date

"Whatever life throws at me I'll take it and be grateful for it as well." – Tom Felton

Today I Am Grateful For

....
....
....
....

Date

What makes you smile?

....

Today I Am Grateful For

....
....
....
....

Date

....
....
....
....

Today I Am Grateful For

Date

What about your upbringing are you most grateful for?

....

Positive Affirmations

....
....
....
....

Today I Am Grateful For

Date

....

....

....

....

....

....

....

....

Today I Am Grateful For

Date

What physical characteristics are you most grateful for?

....

Today I Am Grateful For

Date

....

....

....

....

....

....

....

....

Today I Am Grateful For

Date

"My advice: Take a second out of the day today and be thankful for your family." – Jenna Morasca

Today I Am Grateful For

Date

What is a family tradition that you love?

Today I Am Grateful For

Date

Today I Am Grateful For

Date

Which is worse, failing or never trying?

Positive Affirmations

Today I Am Grateful For

Date

- ....
- ....
- ....
- ....

- ....
- ....
- ....
- ....

Today I Am Grateful For

Date

When was the last time you listened to your own breathing?

....

Today I Am Grateful For

Date

- ....
- ....
- ....
- ....

- ....
- ....
- ....
- ....

Today I Am Grateful For

Date

"I am thankful for all the blessings and talents I have been given, but most of all I am thankful for my loving and supportive family." – Olivia Holt

Today I Am Grateful For

- _____
- _____
- _____
- _____

Date

What's something you do differently than most people?

_____

Today I Am Grateful For

- _____
- _____
- _____
- _____

Date

- _____
- _____
- _____
- _____

Today I Am Grateful For

Date

What is the most desirable trait another person can possess?

_____

Positive Affirmations

- _____
- _____
- _____
- _____

Today I Am Grateful For

Date

Today I Am Grateful For

Date

What are you most grateful for?

Today I Am Grateful For

Date

Today I Am Grateful For

Date

"I'm thankful because all the hard work and sacrifices were worth it in the end." – WizKid

Today I Am Grateful For

- ....
- ....
- ....
- ....

Date

What has life taught you recently?

_____

Today I Am Grateful For

- ....
- ....
- ....
- ....

Date

- ....
- ....
- ....
- ....

Today I Am Grateful For

Date

Where do you find inspiration?

_____

Positive Affirmations

- ....
- ....
- ....
- ....

Today I Am Grateful For

Date

Today I Am Grateful For

Date

What impact do you want to leave on the world?

Today I Am Grateful For

Date

Today I Am Grateful For

Date

"Be thankful for everything that happens in your life; it's all an experience." – Roy T. Bennett

Today I Am Grateful For

_____
_____
_____
_____

Date

Have you ever regretted something you did not say or do?

_____

Today I Am Grateful For

_____
_____
_____
_____

Date

_____
_____
_____
_____

Today I Am Grateful For

Date

What is your most beloved childhood memory?

_____

Positive Affirmations

_____
_____
_____
_____

Today I Am Grateful For

_____
_____
_____
_____

Date

_____
_____
_____
_____

Today I Am Grateful For

Date

Who would you like to please the most?

_____

Today I Am Grateful For

Date

_____
_____
_____
_____

_____
_____
_____
_____

Today I Am Grateful For

Date

"Sometimes the little things in life mean the most." – Ellen Hopkins

Today I Am Grateful For

Date

- _____
- _____
- _____
- _____

Who do you think stands between you and happiness?

_____

Today I Am Grateful For

Date

- _____
- _____
- _____

- _____
- _____
- _____
- _____

Today I Am Grateful For

Date

What gives your life meaning?

_____

Positive Affirmations

- _____
- _____
- _____
- _____

Today I Am Grateful For

Date

Today I Am Grateful For

Date

Are you happy with where you are in your life?

Today I Am Grateful For

Date

Today I Am Grateful For

Date

"I want to thank you for the profound joy I've had in the in the thought of you." – Rosie Alison

Today I Am Grateful For

Date

What is the biggest obstacle that stands in your way right now?

Today I Am Grateful For

Date

Today I Am Grateful For

Date

What makes you feel secure?

Positive Affirmations

Today I Am Grateful For

· ....

· ....

· ....

· ....

Date

♥ ....

♥ ....

♥ ....

♥ ....

Today I Am Grateful For

Date

What do you love most about yourself?

....

Today I Am Grateful For

· ....

· ....

· ....

· ....

Date

♥ ....

♥ ....

♥ ....

♥ ....

Today I Am Grateful For

Date

"Always be thankful for the little things... even the smallest mountains can hide the most breathtaking views." – Nyki Mack

Today I Am Grateful For

Date

- ♥
- ♥
- ♥
- ♥

What do you have that you cannot live without?

Today I Am Grateful For

Date

- ♥
- ♥
- ♥
- ♥

Today I Am Grateful For

Date

- ♥
- ♥
- ♥
- ♥

When you close your eyes what do you see

Positive Affirmations

- ♥
- ♥
- ♥
- ♥

Today I Am Grateful For

Date

Today I Am Grateful For

Date

What sustains you on a daily basis?

Today I Am Grateful For

Date

Today I Am Grateful For

Date

"A little 'thank you' that you will say to someone for a 'little favor' shown to you is a key to unlock the doors that hide unseen 'greater favors'." – Israelmore Ayivor

Today I Am Grateful For

Date

_____

_____
_____
_____
_____

What are your top five personal values?

_____

Today I Am Grateful For

Date

_____
_____
_____
_____

_____
_____
_____
_____

Today I Am Grateful For

Date

Why must you love someone enough to let them go?

_____

Positive Affirmations

_____
_____
_____
_____

Today I Am Grateful For

Date

Today I Am Grateful For

Date

What one thing have you not done that you really want to do?

Today I Am Grateful For

Date

Today I Am Grateful For

Date

"What am I most thankful for? LOVE! Because without it, I wouldn't have a life." – Anthony T. Hincks

Today I Am Grateful For

Date

- ....
- ....
- ....
- ....

What are the top three qualities you look for in a friend?

_____

Today I Am Grateful For

Date

- ....
- ....
- ....
- ....

- ....
- ....
- ....
- ....

Today I Am Grateful For

Date

How would you describe 'freedom' in your own words?

_____

Positive Affirmations

- ....
- ....
- ....
- ....

Today I Am Grateful For

_____

Date

Today I Am Grateful For

_____

Date

What do you love to do?

Today I Am Grateful For

_____

Date

Today I Am Grateful For

_____

Date

"Never regret a day in your life. Good days give happiness, bad days give experience, worst days give lessons, and best days give memories."

Today I Am Grateful For

Date

- ....
- ....
- ....
- ....

What is your number one goal for the next six months?

....

Today I Am Grateful For

Date

- ....
- ....
- ....
- ....

- ....
- ....
- ....
- ....

Today I Am Grateful For

Date

Are you happy with yourself?

....

Positive Affirmations

- ....
- ....
- ....
- ....

Today I Am Grateful For

Date

- ....
- ....
- ....
- ....

- ....
- ....
- ....
- ....

Today I Am Grateful For

Date

What does it mean to allow another person to truly love you?

....

Today I Am Grateful For

Date

- ....
- ....
- ....
- ....

- ....
- ....
- ....
- ....

Today I Am Grateful For

Date

"When asked if my cup is half-full or half empty, my only response is that I am thankful I have a cup."

Today I Am Grateful For

- ....
- ....
- ....

Date

Who or what do you think of when you think of love?

....

Today I Am Grateful For

- ....
- ....
- ....

Date

- ....
- ....
- ....

Today I Am Grateful For

Date

When do you feel most like yourself?

....

Positive Affirmations

- ....
- ....
- ....
- ....

Today I Am Grateful For

Date

Today I Am Grateful For

Date

How do you define success?

Today I Am Grateful For

Date

Today I Am Grateful For

Date

"Be thankful for the struggles you go through. They make you stronger, wiser and humble. Don't let them break you. Let them make you."

Today I Am Grateful For

Date

- _____
- _____
- _____
- _____

What have you read online recently that inspired you?

_____

Today I Am Grateful For

Date

- _____
- _____
- _____
- _____

- _____
- _____
- _____
- _____

Today I Am Grateful For

Date

What specific character trait do you want to be known for?

_____

Positive Affirmations

- _____
- _____
- _____
- _____

Today I Am Grateful For

....

....

....

....

Date

....

....

....

....

Today I Am Grateful For

Date

What is the one thing that made me smile today?

....

Today I Am Grateful For

....

....

....

....

Date

....

....

....

....

Today I Am Grateful For

Date

"Happiness isn't about getting what you want all the time. It's about loving what you have and being grateful for it."

Today I Am Grateful For

♥ ....
♥ ....
♥ ....
♥ ....

Date

What is the one thing that made me smile today?

....

Today I Am Grateful For

♥ ....
♥ ....
♥ ....
♥ ....

Date

♥ ....
♥ ....
♥ ....
♥ ....

Today I Am Grateful For

Date

What is the one thing that made me smile today?

....

Positive Affirmations
♥♥♥

♥ ....
♥ ....
♥ ....
♥ ....

Today I Am Grateful For

Date

Today I Am Grateful For

Date

What makes everyone smile?

Today I Am Grateful For

Date

Today I Am Grateful For

Date

"Be thankful for what you have. Your life, no matter how bad you think it is, is someone else's fairytale."

Today I Am Grateful For

Date

....
....
....
....

What do you owe yourself?

....

Today I Am Grateful For

Date

....
....
....
....

....
....
....
....

Today I Am Grateful For

Date

How have you changed in the last five years?

....

Positive Affirmations

....
....
....
....

Today I Am Grateful For

Date

Today I Am Grateful For

Date

What are you sure of in your life?

Today I Am Grateful For

Date

Today I Am Grateful For

Date

"A grateful heart is a magnet for miracles."

Today I Am Grateful For

Date

- ....
- ....
- ....
- ....

When you think of 'home,' what, specifically, do you think of?

....

Today I Am Grateful For

Date

- ....
- ....
- ....
- ....

- ....
- ....
- ....
- ....

Today I Am Grateful For

Date

What is your most prized possession?

....

Positive Affirmations

- ....
- ....
- ....
- ....

Today I Am Grateful For

Date

Today I Am Grateful For

Date

How would you describe yourself in one sentence?

Today I Am Grateful For

Date

Today I Am Grateful For

Date

"Upon waking, let your first thought be, Thank you."

Today I Am Grateful For

Date

- ....
- ....
- ....
- ....

What makes you proud?

....

Today I Am Grateful For

Date

- ....
- ....
- ....
- ....

- ....
- ....
- ....
- ....

Today I Am Grateful For

Date

When does silence convey more meaning than words?

....

Positive Affirmations

- ....
- ....
- ....
- ....

Today I Am Grateful For

Date

. . . .

. . . .

. . . .

. . . .

Today I Am Grateful For

Date

How do you spend the majority of your free time?

_____

Today I Am Grateful For

Date

Today I Am Grateful For

Date

"Replace expectation with gratitude."

Today I Am Grateful For

Date

_____

Who do you think of first when you think of success?

_____

Today I Am Grateful For

Date

_____

Today I Am Grateful For

Date

What did you want to be when you grew up?

_____

Positive Affirmations

Today I Am Grateful For

- ....
- ....
- ....
- ....

Date

- ....
- ....
- ....
- ....

Today I Am Grateful For

Date

How will today matter in five years from now?

....

Today I Am Grateful For

- ....
- ....
- ....
- ....

Date

- ....
- ....
- ....
- ....

Today I Am Grateful For

Date

"The secret of being happy is accepting where you are in life and making the most of every day."

Today I Am Grateful For

Date

How have you helped someone else recently?

Today I Am Grateful For

Date

Today I Am Grateful For

Date

What are you looking forward to?

Positive Affirmations

Today I Am Grateful For

Date

- ....
- ....
- ....
- ....

- ....
- ....
- ....
- ....

Today I Am Grateful For

Date

Who is the strongest person you know?

....

Today I Am Grateful For

Date

- ....
- ....
- ....
- ....

- ....
- ....
- ....

Today I Am Grateful For

Date

"I'm thankful for my struggle because without it I wouldn't have stumbled across my strength."

Today I Am Grateful For

Date

....
....
....
....

What have you done in the last year that makes you proud?

_____

Today I Am Grateful For

Date

....
....
....
....

....
....
....
....

Today I Am Grateful For

Date

What is your fondest memory from the past three years?

_____

Positive Affirmations

....
....
....
....

Today I Am Grateful For

Date

Today I Am Grateful For

Date

What is your favorite song and why?

Today I Am Grateful For

Date

Today I Am Grateful For

Date

"Remember that life's greatest lessons are usually learned at the worst times and from the worst mistakes."

Today I Am Grateful For

- ....
- ....
- ....
- ....

Date

What can you do to bring yourself closer to your goal?

....

Today I Am Grateful For

- ....
- ....
- ....
- ....

Date

- ....
- ....
- ....
- ....

Today I Am Grateful For

Date

What are your top three priorities?

....

Positive Affirmations

- ....
- ....
- ....
- ....

Today I Am Grateful For

Date

Today I Am Grateful For

Date

What do you see when you look into the future?

Today I Am Grateful For

Date

Today I Am Grateful For

Date

"Remember when you prayed for the things you have now."

Today I Am Grateful For

Date

What makes you angry? Why?

Today I Am Grateful For

Date

Today I Am Grateful For

Date

What valuable life lesson you learned from your parents?

Positive Affirmations

Today I Am Grateful For

♥ ....
♥ ....
♥ ....
♥ ....

Date

♥ ....
♥ ....
♥ ....
♥ ....

Today I Am Grateful For

Date

What is your earliest childhood memory?

_____

Today I Am Grateful For

♥ ....
♥ ....
♥ ....
♥ ....

Date

♥ ....
♥ ....
♥ ....
♥ ....

Today I Am Grateful For

Date

"Gratitude means to recognize the good in your life, be thankful for whatever you have, some people may not even have one of those things you consider precious to you." – Pablo

Today I Am Grateful For

- _____
- _____
- _____
- _____

Date

Excluding romantic relationships, who do you love?

_____

Today I Am Grateful For

- _____
- _____
- _____
- _____

Date

- _____
- _____
- _____
- _____

Today I Am Grateful For

Date

What do you think is worth waiting for?

_____

Positive Affirmations

- _____
- _____
- _____
- _____

Today I Am Grateful For

Date

Today I Am Grateful For

Date

What is your greatest strength and your greatest weakness?

Today I Am Grateful For

Date

Today I Am Grateful For

Date

"Each of us has cause to think with deep gratitude of those who have lighted the flame within us." — Albert Schweitzer

Today I Am Grateful For

Date

- ♥
- ♥
- ♥
- ♥

What made you smile this week?

Today I Am Grateful For

Date

- ♥
- ♥
- ♥

Today I Am Grateful For

Date

What will you never give up on?

Positive Affirmations

- ♥
- ♥
- ♥
- ♥

Today I Am Grateful For

- _____
- _____
- _____
- _____

Date

- _____
- _____
- _____
- _____

Today I Am Grateful For

Date

When you look into the past, what do you miss the most?

_____

Today I Am Grateful For

- _____
- _____
- _____
- _____

Date

- _____
- _____
- _____
- _____

Today I Am Grateful For

Date

"Nothing is a coincidence. Everything you're experiencing is meant to happen exactly how it's happening. Embrace the lessons. Be grateful."

Today I Am Grateful For

Date

- ....
- ....
- ....
- ....

What makes you uncomfortable?

_____

Today I Am Grateful For

Date

- ....
- ....
- ....
- ....

- ....
- ....
- ....
- ....

Today I Am Grateful For

Date

What's the best part of being you?

_____

Positive Affirmations

- ....
- ....
- ....
- ....

Today I Am Grateful For

Date

....
....
....
....

....
....
....
....

Today I Am Grateful For

Date

What artistic medium do you use to express yourself?

_____

Today I Am Grateful For

Date

....
....
....
....

....
....
....
....

Today I Am Grateful For

Date

"Always be thankful for what you have. Many people have nothing."

Today I Am Grateful For

Date

- _____
- _____
- _____
- _____

What do you do to relieve stress?

_____

Today I Am Grateful For

Date

- _____
- _____
- _____
- _____

- _____
- _____
- _____
- _____

Today I Am Grateful For

Date

What is your happiest memory?

_____

Positive Affirmations

- _____
- _____
- _____
- _____

Today I Am Grateful For

-
-
-
-

Date

-
-
-
-

Today I Am Grateful For

Date

What would you like to change (about yourself)?

Today I Am Grateful For

Date

-
-
-
-

-
-
-

Today I Am Grateful For

Date

"Enjoy the little things, for one day you may look back and realize they were the big things."

—Robert Brault

Today I Am Grateful For

Date

....

....

....

....

What's the best decision you've ever made?

....

Today I Am Grateful For

Date

....

....

....

....

....

....

....

....

Today I Am Grateful For

Date

Right now, at this moment, what do you want most?

....

Positive Affirmations

....

....

....

....

Today I Am Grateful For

Date

Today I Am Grateful For

Date

What's the most important lesson you've learned last year?

Today I Am Grateful For

Date

Today I Am Grateful For

Date

"We should certainly count our blessings, but we should also make our blessings count."

—Neal A. Maxwell

Today I Am Grateful For

Date

- _____
- _____
- _____
- _____

What do you think about when you lie awake in bed?

_____

Today I Am Grateful For

Date

- _____
- _____
- _____
- _____

- _____
- _____
- _____
- _____

Today I Am Grateful For

Date

What are you uncertain about?

_____

Positive Affirmations

- _____
- _____
- _____
- _____

Today I Am Grateful For

....
....
....
....

Date

....
....
....
....

Today I Am Grateful For

Date

What did life teach you yesterday?

....

Today I Am Grateful For

....
....
....
....

Date

....
....
....
....

Today I Am Grateful For

Date

"Acknowledging the good that you already have in your life is the foundation for all abundance." – Eckhart Tolle

—Eckhart Tolle

Today I Am Grateful For

Date

- ....
- ....
- ....
- ....

What positive changes have you made in your life recently?

....

Today I Am Grateful For

Date

- ....
- ....
- ....
- ....

- ....
- ....
- ....
- ....

Today I Am Grateful For

Date

Who makes you feel good about yourself?

....

Positive Affirmations

- ....
- ....
- ....
- ....

Today I Am Grateful For

Date

♥ ....
♥ ....
♥ ....
♥ ....

Today I Am Grateful For

Date

♥ ....
♥ ....
♥ ....
♥ ....

What do you want more of in your life?

_____

Today I Am Grateful For

Date

♥ ....
♥ ....
♥ ....
♥ ....

♥ ....
♥ ....
♥ ....
♥ ....

Today I Am Grateful For

Date

"A thankful heart is not only the greatest virtue, but the parent of all the other virtues." – Cicero

—Cicero

Today I Am Grateful For

Date

- _____
- _____
- _____
- _____

What do you want less of in your life?
_____

Today I Am Grateful For

Date

- _____
- _____
- _____
- _____

- _____
- _____
- _____

Today I Am Grateful For

Date

Who has had the greatest impact on your life?
_____

Positive Affirmations

- _____
- _____
- _____
- _____

Thank you for purchasing this book. If you enjoyed using this book, then feedback on amazon would be greatly appreciated. It would be really kind of you to take the time to write a review, which would help us immensely.

For any suggestions or questions regarding our book please contact us at the email below.
To join our mailing list for our latest book releases & early bird discounts email us with
Subject- 'Gratitude Journal' @
oceanicbookhub@gmail.com

Without your voice we don't exist.
Thank you for your support.

Notes & Thoughts

Made in the USA
Columbia, SC
01 June 2023

17590103R00065